MATH
RIDDLES
&
BRAIN
TEASERS

For Kids 10+

UNICORN BOOKS

INTRODUCTION

This book consists of 60 challenging math brain teasers. You will discover the power of simple (but not trivial) math concepts when applied to real-world situations.

Some unique features of this book include:

- **Colorful illustrations** on every page.
- **Hints for every puzzle.** If you are stuck, you don't have to give up. A small hint will help you move forward.
- **Full solutions and explanations.** Enrich your mathematical toolkit with every puzzle.
- **Increasing levels of difficulty.** From warm-up riddles to extremely tricky ones. But it is not necessary to follow a strict order. Flip through the pages and let yourself be inspired by the titles and images in choosing your next puzzle.
- **Creative mathematical challenges.** In the boxes labeled "The Little Mathematician" you will be prompted to invent your own riddles or guided in discovering more advanced mathematical formulas. You will wander into the unknown, like a true mathematician!

The Little Mathematician

Express your creativity through mathematics

This book was designed to be at the same time challenging, entertaining, and fun. The brain teasers do not require any advanced knowledge and use only elementary math. But do not underestimate them. They can be hard for people of any age and level of instruction. Don't believe me? Try them on your parents, your older siblings, or even your teachers.

You will notice that the more puzzles you tackle, the better you will get at solving them. That's because you are improving your ability to think outside the box, which is useful in every aspect of your life!

Before we start...

If you wish to support our work and would like to see more books like this one available, consider leaving your honest review on Amazon.

If you like logic puzzles, you should also check out our book *Logic Grid Puzzles & Other Games*.

And now... Let the fun begin!

1. SECRET CODE

The code to open my padlock consists of three digits.

- The sum of all three is equal to 10.
- The product of the first two equals 6.
- The second digit is the highest.

What is the code that opens the padlock?

2. MYSTERIOUS WEIGHT

The scale below is perfectly balanced. We have the following information:
- Four of the weights measure, respectively, 2 lb, 3 lb, 5 lb, and 10 lb.
- Two out of the five weights are equal.

How heavy is the fifth weight?

3. PERFECT BBQ

Frank is a BBQ master. To obtain a perfect steak, he grills each side for five minutes.

Tonight, Frank wants to prepare three steaks, but unfortunately on his grill there is space for at most two steaks.

How long will it take Frank, at minimum, to grill three steaks on both sides?

4. GIGANTIC PRODUCTS

The math teacher wrote on the blackboard the following scary calculation.

$$2 \times 4 \times 6 \times 8 \times .... \times 2022$$

It is the product of all the even numbers from 2 to 2022. She then asks the following questions to her students.

What is the last digit of the result?
And the one before last?

5. CHALLENGE FROM THE DESERT

In this piece of papyrus found in the desert, a sum was calculated.

We can distinguish the digit 1 in the result of the operation.

Find out what digits the two symbols are replacing.

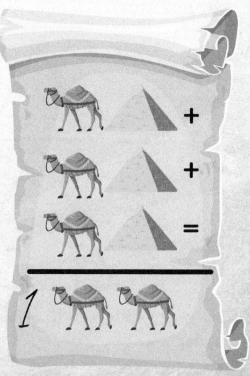

6. SWEET BREAKFAST

Yesterday I went to a French patisserie with my friends Alyssa and Jasmine. Alyssa ordered one croissant and two cappuccinos, spending $6.60.

Jasmine got two croissants and one cappuccino. She spent $6. I ordered one croissant and one cappuccino.

How much did I spend?

7. TRIANGULAR CAT

James, who likes both geometry and animals, has produced the following drawing of a cat.

How many different triangles can you count in James's drawing?

8. CROWDED BUS

Today, when I got on the bus, I counted 13 other passengers. At the first stop, 10 more passengers got on the bus.

At the following stop, half of the passengers got off. At the stop after that, I got off, and so did 11 other passengers.

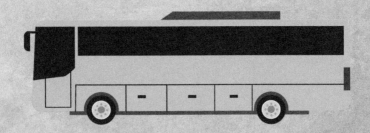

How many people were left on the bus, at that point?

9. MANY SIBLINGS

Laura is a young girl who loves math riddles and logic puzzles.

Today she noticed the following peculiar fact. In her family, each child can say to have at least one brother and one sister.

How many brothers and sisters does Laura have at minimum?

10. SPIDER'S WEBS

To move between two branches of a tree, Steve the spider has built an intricate web. The web consists of 22 pieces, each stretched between two leaves of the tree.

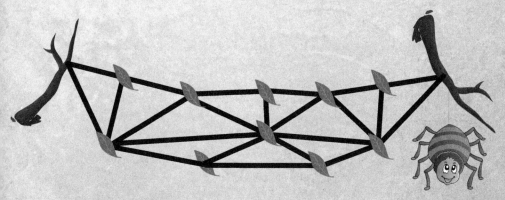

After a violent storm, Steve can still move between the two branches walking on what is left of his web.

How many pieces of the web were destroyed by the storm, at most?

11. SONGWRITERS

Pedro and Camila form an enthusiastic music duo and only perform their own original songs.

Their repertoire consists of a total of eight songs. Pedro contributed to five of them, while Camila to six.

How many of their eight songs did they write together?

12. EVEN AND ODD

Complete the two sentences to make them true statements. (Careful because the numbers you write are also inside the rectangle).

1	2	3	4

Inside this rectangle there are .... odd numbers.

5			6

Inside this rectangle there are .... even numbers.

7	8	9	10

What numbers should be written in place of the dots?

13. CURIOUS BIRTHDAYS

In a group of friends, everyone has a different birthday. Still, they all have something in common: to write the day and month of birth of every friend, one never needs the digits 4, 5, 6, 7, 8, or 9.

What is the maximum number of friends in that group?

14. LACK OF CASH

Marina and Robert would like to buy a new comic book. They search their pockets and find some one-dollar bills.

> I can't buy it. I am missing 2 dollars.

> I can't buy it either. I am missing 6 dollars.

Neither of the two friends is without money. However, even when they put their dollar bills together, they don't have enough money to make the purchase.

What is the price of the comic book?

15. GLOVES OBSESSION

Samantha has 60 pairs of gloves in her drawer. They are in 5 different colors, 12 pairs for each color. Since the lights are out, she is in complete darkness.

She wants to make sure she picks at least one pair of the same color.

What is the minimum number of gloves that she should take out of the drawer?

16. MATHEMATICAL WONDERS

Julia has just discovered two three-digit numbers with a surprising property: they are equal to the sum of the third powers of their digits. Here is what she wrote on the blackboard to explain her discovery.

$$153 = 1^3 + 5^3 + 3^3$$
$$370 = 3^3 + 7^3 + 0^3$$

Starting from Julie's numbers, it is possible to find, without any calculations, another three-digit number with the same property. **What is this number?**

17. HUNGRY MONKEYS

Seven monkeys eat seven bananas in seven minutes.

How many monkeys will eat 98 bananas in 49 minutes?

18. THREE SPECIAL NUMBERS

These three numbers give the same result whether they are added together or multiplied.

What are these three special numbers?

19. STAYING HYDRATED

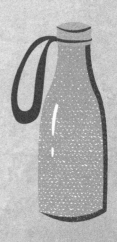

Daniel's bottle now weighs 1.2 lb, but it is only half full of water.

When the bottle is completely filled with water, it weighs 2 lb.

What is the weight of the empty bottle?

20. OLD FRIENDS

Frank, Anthony, Daniel, and Robert have been friends since childhood. Frank is older than Daniel, who is older than Anthony. The sum of the ages of Anthony and Robert is greater than the sum of the ages of Daniel and Frank.

Who is the oldest in the group? Who is the youngest?

21. IMPERFECT CUTTING

Nancy cut a round pizza into eleven pieces making only straight cuts and without folding the pizza. She is quite disappointed by the result: all the pieces have different shapes and sizes!

What a mess! But she was just trying to save time, making the minimum possible number of cuts so that she and her ten friends could each have a piece.

How many cuts did Nancy make?

22. PRESIDENTIAL RIDDLE

Simon is quoting from his trivia book. "Did you know that of the first five US presidents (in order, Washington, Adams, Jefferson, Madison, and Monroe) three died on the fourth of July?"

Lucy replies "I have never heard this before, but I am ready to bet my lunch money that Monroe is one of those three."

How can Lucy be so sure?

23. UNRELIABLE ANTS

In a remote corner of the globe, there are three types of ants. The red ones always lie but are honest on the last two days of every month. The green ants always tell the truth, except during the days ending with a zero (that is, 10, 20, or 30). In those days, they always lie. The yellow ants lie on even days and are truthful on odd days.

One day in November I could not remember the exact date, so I asked three ants, "Is today the 30th?". Here are their replies.

Yes, it is the 30th.

At least two of us are lying.

No, it isn't. Today is the 29th.

Today is definitely not an even day.

On which day did this conversation take place?

24. SPORT WITH FRIENDS

Christian would like to celebrate his birthday by going out with his friends. He is considering two different options.

He could take 10 friends to a basketball game, or he could take his 4 closest friends to 5 different hockey games. Obviously, Christian wants to pay for everyone's tickets, including his own.

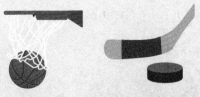

Knowing that a ticket for a basketball game costs twice as much as a ticket for a hockey game, which option is cheaper?

25. DIFFICULT MEASUREMENTS

Michael wants to measure the height of his table. Unfortunately, his two favorite pets, Flippy the turtle and Bandit the cat, keep getting in the way. Here are the measurements he was able to carry out.

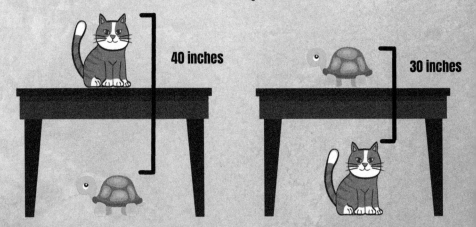

40 inches

30 inches

What is the height of the table?

26. CORDIAL GATHERING

At the end of a party every participant shook hands with everyone else. There were 9 people at the party.

How many handshakes were exchanged?

27. SOCCER CUP

Chelsea has just won a tough game against Juventus.
The final score was 7 - 5. At half-time, Chelsea had scored as many goals as Juventus later scored during the second half.

How many of the 12 total goals were scored during the first half of the game?

28. MEASURING TIME

You have two hourglasses in front of you. The first hourglass measures 7 minutes, while the other one measures 4 minutes.

How is it possible for you to measure exactly nine minutes using only these two hourglasses?

29. LOST BANKNOTE

At the library, I opened a book and a twenty-dollar bill fell out. Immediately, a woman behind me said, "It's mine. I was using it as a bookmark. I left it between the pages 124 and 125."

Another man entered the conversation, saying, "It's mine! I left it between pages 201 and 202".

I checked the book and saw that it had 246 pages.

To whom did I give the banknote?

30. THIRSTY CAMELS

Five Bactrian camels drink 5 gallons of water in 5 days.
Seven Arabian camels drink 7 gallons of water in 7 days.

Which of the two species requires a higher daily amount of water?

31. WALL PAINTING

Levin is an expert painter. He paints an entire wall in three hours. Alex is still an apprentice, and it takes him six hours to do the same job.

Today, they started to paint a wall together.

How long will it take them to complete the task?

32. ERASE AND WRITE

Lee wrote on the blackboard all the numbers from 1 to 10.

$$1 - 2 - 3 - 4 - 5$$
$$6 - 7 - 8 - 9 - 10$$

He now starts the following process: he chooses two numbers and erases them from the blackboard, replacing them with their sum increased by one. For instance, if he chooses 3 and 8, he erases them and writes 12 somewhere on the blackboard.

Lee keeps repeating this procedure until there is only one number left on the blackboard.

What is this number?

33. READY FOR THANKSGIVING

In a community of 20 turkey farmers, each farmer has 1, 5, or 9 turkeys.

The number of farmers who have 1 turkey is equal to the number of farmers who have 9 turkeys.

How many turkeys are raised in that community?

34. THREATENING QUEENS

You want to place three chess queens on a 3×3 chessboard so that no two queens threaten each other. That is, a solution requires that no two queens share the same row, column, or diagonal.

Can you solve this problem?
What if the queens are 4 on a 4x4 chessboard?

35. LAND DIVISION

A farmer divided his land into four equal rectangular pieces.

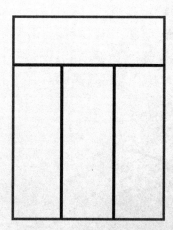

Each piece is enclosed by 160 ft of fence.

What is the total area of the land?

36. THREE CURIOUS FRIENDS

Jennifer, Linda, and Thomas are three adventurous friends looking for interesting insects and beetles in the forest.

Jennifer and Linda together found 27 insects, Thomas and Jennifer 30, and Thomas and Linda 33.

How many did they find in total? Who found more?

37. PICK AND SUM

Ethan is in front of a giant urn containing balls numbered from 13 to 2021, one ball for each number. He picks blindfolded two balls at the same time and then sums the two numbers on the balls.

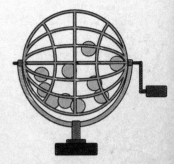

Here is an example.

125 **+** 1093 **=** 1218

How many different sums can Ethan obtain?

38. APPLES AND ORANGES

All my apples weigh the same as each other. All my oranges weigh the same as each other. Here are two situations in which the scale is perfectly balanced.

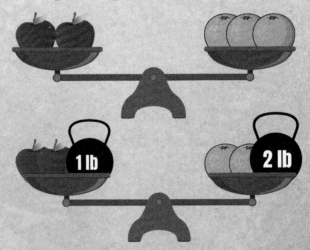

What is the weight of an apple?

39. TIES ALLOWED

Caleb, Taylor and Lucy are running a race against each other. It is possible to tie for first or second place.

In how many different ways can the race end?

40. STRANGE PLANETS

On the planet Gok the inhabitants move in a strange way. They take three steps forward and then two backward along the same line. Quke, an inhabitant of Gok, has walked a total of 100 steps in the same direction starting from his front door.

How many steps away is he now from the door?

41. GAME OF MARBLES

Daniel and Andrew are playing marbles. When one of them loses a game, he gives the other as many marbles as the winner has at that moment. Therefore, when one wins, he doubles the number of marbles in his possession. After playing three games, both Daniel and Andrew own 56 marbles. Moreover, neither of them won two games in a row.

How many marbles did the two friends have before the first game?

42. FAST FOOD

Today Matthew got a cheeseburger with fries for lunch.
He thought about ordering onion rings as a side instead, but those cost three times as much as the fries. For the cheeseburger and onion rings he would have had to pay $13. Instead, by getting the regular fries, he spent a total of $9.

What is the price of a cheeseburger?

43. OUT FOR A WALK

Emily wants to visit her friend Michelle. It's a sunny day, so she decides to walk to her friend's house. Unfortunately, when she is halfway there, it starts raining. She decides to go back home to get an umbrella.

Halfway through her journey back, the sun starts shining again. She then turns around to continue to Michelle's house. When she finally arrives at her friend's place, she has walked a total of 12 miles.

What is the distance between Emily's house and Michelle's?

44. CURSED TREASURE

A crew of 20 pirates has just found on an island a treasure consisting of a large number of golden doubloons. At first, they divide the doubloons equally among themselves.

On the way back to the ship, four men are eaten by crocodiles. Eight more are killed during a storm while trying to leave the island. The dead men's share of the treasure is redistributed equally among the survivors. On the first night on the boat one drunk pirate falls into the sea bringing with him his share of doubloons.

Before they get to their destination, two more pirates perish after catching a fatal disease. The few surviving pirates then divide equally among themselves the doubloons of these two dead men. Now they have 350 doubloons each.

How many doubloons did each pirate have after the initial distribution of the treasure?

45. FLYING CARDS

Mark accidentally left his window open, and a sudden gust of wind made his collection of 120 baseball cards fly away.

To recover them, he published an ad in the newspaper offering a reward to anyone who would find and bring back a certain specified number of baseball cards.

Three people showed up at Mark's door. None of them got the reward, because none of them had the number of cards specified in the ad.

The first person was missing two, the second person was missing four, while the third person still needed six cards to get the reward.

However, Mark was happy because together the three people had recovered all his 120 baseball cards.

How many cards were needed to receive the reward?

46. HOSPITABLE ISLAND

After a storm destroyed their ship, three pirates become stranded on an almost-deserted island. Nobody lives on that island except Peanut the dog. Among the wreckage of their ship, the pirates have just found a box with some cookies. They decide to eat them the following morning for breakfast.

Being pirates, they know better than to trust each other. The first pirate gets up in the middle of the night and goes for the cookies. To keep Peanut quiet, the pirate gives him a cookie, then eats half of the content of the box. Later that night, the second pirate does the same thing: he gives one cookie to Peanut and then eats half of the cookies left in the box.

Finally, the third pirate goes through the same sequence of actions. In the morning, the pirates eat one cookie each and then toss the last cookie to Peanut. At that point, the box is empty.

How many cookies were in the box when the pirates found it?

47. EFFICIENT CHAINS

Mark the blacksmith has four pieces of chain, each consisting of three rings. He wants to obtain a single round chain as in the picture.

It takes Mark a minute to open a ring and another minute to close it.

How long will it take Mark to complete this task, at minimum?

48. FAST SALES

Today was a profitable day for Gloria. She got to the market with her load of watermelons early in the morning, but after two hours she had already sold everything.

The first customer bought half of her watermelons. The second one bought one third of the remaining fruits. The third customer asked for five watermelons, but Gloria gave him an additional one for free, so that she had no watermelons left and could go home.

How many watermelons did Gloria have at the beginning of the day?

49. STOLEN BERRIES

Kayla walks home after an afternoon spent looking for wild berries. She is quite happy because she has improved on the 16 berries found yesterday. However, she still hasn't been able to beat her brother's record of 40.

Once home, Kayla leaves her basket containing strawberries and blueberries on the doorstep and goes inside to say hi to her mom.

When she returns outside to get her basket, she finds an unpleasant surprise waiting for her. A bird has eaten 2 out of every 7 of her berries! Now, she notices, she has as many strawberries as she has blueberries.

How many berries were in Kayla's basket when she got home?

50. BEDTIME STORY

Every night, grandma reads to Sydney part of a fantasy novel. The book they are currently enjoying is 96 pages long.

Grandma usually goes through at least 10 pages in one night. Tonight, however, Sydney is exhausted, and grandma manages to read only two pages before Sydney falls soundly asleep. The sum of the digits of the numbers of the two pages is 24.

What pages did grandma read that night?

51. GROWING BACTERIA

Matilde is a scientist working on a newly discovered species of bacteria. These bacteria triple in number (and therefore in volume occupied) every thirty minutes.

At 8 am Matilde puts a single bacterium in a test tube. At 5 pm the test tube is completely filled with bacteria.

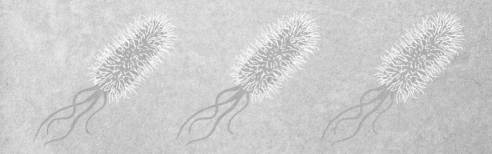

At what time would the test tube have been full if Matilde had put three bacteria in the test tube instead of a single one?

52. WEEKEND IN SPACE

Five spaceships left the planet Gok for a weekend trip to another corner of the galaxy. Unfortunately, on the way back, one collides with an unidentified object, resulting in an engine failure. Its passengers, therefore, transfer to the other vehicles. They do it so that each of the remaining spaceships will have the same total number of passengers.

Since the four undamaged ships had respectively 17, 19, 14, and 22 passengers, how many people were traveling in the fifth spaceship, at minimum?

53. SCOUTING CAMPAIGN

Misty has been instructed to conduct a three-hour scouting campaign. To move faster, she leaves her backpack behind with her group, which will be following her along the same path. Without the weight of the backpack, Misty moves at the constant speed of 6 miles per hour, while her platoon advances behind her in the same direction at the speed of 4 miles per hour.

After how long will Misty have to turn around to meet the rest of her company exactly three hours after she left them?

54. CHEERFUL BIRDS

The big cherry tree in my garden is home to many birds. This morning I observed several Robins and Cardinals on its branches.

Suddenly, my dog started barking. Eight Robins got scared and flew away. Five of them later came back. When my dad started his car, three Cardinals went away. After a few minutes, two came back to the tree.

At that point, I counted a total of 13 birds on the tree.

How many Robins were on the tree initially, at most?

55. BIRTHDAY PARTY

Patrick is turning ten in a few days, and he has invited nine good friends to celebrate with him. He stares at the list of guests and notices a peculiar fact.

The fist guest only knows one of the ten people who will be present at the birthday party (and that person, of course, is Patrick). The second guest knows two, the third guest three, and so on until the eighth guest, who knows eight. The ninth guest is Lauren.

How many of the people who will be at the party does Lauren know?

56. MATH MAGICIAN

Yesterday at school, Malika told me she had developed incredible mathematical abilities and wanted to give me a demonstration.

She asked me for three numbers smaller than 10,000. I gave her 5482, 1450, and 2307. After writing them on the board, she asked our friend Lucas for two more numbers. He gave her 4517 and 8549. Malika had barely finished writing these two when she exclaimed "The sum of the five numbers is 22,305." I checked with the calculator, and it turned out she was right.

I was genuinely impressed, but also a bit suspicious. So, I asked her to repeat the game. This time, I gave Malika the numbers 1799, 2005, and 3580. When I heard Lucas saying 8200 and 7994, my suspicions were confirmed. Malika and Lucas had conspired to fool me, and I knew exactly how they were pulling it off.

Can you understand how Lucas and Malika's trick works?

57. ASTEROID IMPACT

The Earth is in danger! A massive asteroid is travelling toward our planet at the speed of 9 miles per second. Luckily, scientists and engineers at the EADD (Earth Asteroid Defense Department) have been working on a new defensive technology, giving us some chances of survival. They have built a special rocket ship that will be launched from the spot of foreseen impact of the asteroid. It will travel upward at an average speed of 3 miles per second and deliberately crash itself into the asteroid to divert its path.

Scientists wish it would be possible to hit the asteroid when it is far away from the planet. However, for maximum accuracy, they have decided that the impact with the rocket ship should occur only 6 miles from the Earth's surface, when the asteroid is about to enter our planet's atmosphere.

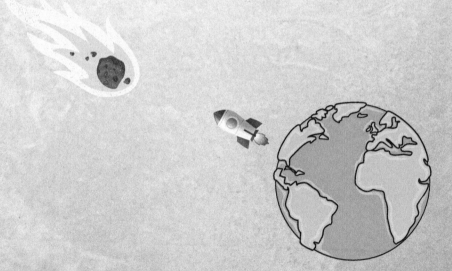

How far away from the Earth will the asteroid be when the head of the EADD pushes the button to initiate the 10 second countdown for the launch?

58. MARTIAN MISSION

Rick and Miranda are the most daring astronauts of the 25th human mission to Mars. This time they have decided to climb Olympus Mons. Standing almost 70,000 feet above the surface of the planet, it is the highest and most impressive mountain on Mars. The astronauts start the mission with two backpacks of the same exact weight.

During the ascent, they stop to rest and admire the takeoff of a spaceship. While on this break, they eat all the food from Miranda's backpack, which as a result weighs one third less than Rick's. Rick then transfers some equipment to Miranda's backpack so that the two are once again carrying the same weight. On their second break, they eat from Rick's backpack, which as a result is now three quarters the weight of Miranda's backpack, that is, 2 lb less.

What was the weight of the two backpacks when Rick and Miranda started their ascent of Olympus Mons?

59. HUNGRY PUPPIES

Isabella has four puppies named Diesel, Tank, Rocket, and Rambo. She is about to treat them with some delicious croquettes. Diesel, who is the most voracious, will receive 140 croquettes, while Tank, Rocket, and Rambo will get 120 croquettes each. Diesel, however, eats much faster than the others. He devours a croquette every second, while Tank, Rocket, and Rambo, each eat a croquette every two seconds.

When one puppy is done with his share, it will keep eating at the same speed but from the bowl of one of the others. This goes on until all the food is gone. The four dogs start tucking into their croquettes all at the same time.

How many seconds will it take the puppies to finish all the food?

60. DESERT CROSSING

Beatrix must cross a dangerous desert with her jeep. The drive, if done without breaks, takes five hours. However, the jeep can only drive for one hour with a full tank of fuel. Luckily, Beatrix has plenty of additional fuel tanks at the base camp from where she is starting the trip. Each tank contains fuel for one hour of driving.

Unfortunately, Beatrix cannot carry more than two additional tanks of fuel in the car, since the extra weight would cause the jeep to get stuck in the sand.
Beatrix understands that the only way for her to be able to make the crossing is to drive ahead and deposit some fuel tanks along the way, then drive back and pick up more tanks.

How long will it take Beatrix at least to cross the desert?

HINTS

1. SECRET CODE

Start from the information on the product.

2. MYSTERIOUS WEIGHT

The sum of the four given weights is 2+3+5+10=20 lb.
If we add the fifth weight, we must obtain an **even** number (since it is possible to split the total weight equally between the two sides of the scale).

3. PERFECT BBQ

It is not necessary for the two sides of a steak to be grilled consecutively one after the other.

4. GIGANTIC PRODUCTS

When the numbers seem too big, it is useful to work on a simplified version of the problem. Instead of going all the way to 2022, try to compute the following simpler products.

2x4

2x4x6

2x4x6x8

2x4x6x8x10

2x4x6x8x10x12

For the moment, you only need to pay attention to the last digit. Do you notice anything?

5. CHALLENGE FROM THE DESERT

It is convenient to start by assigning a value to the pyramid. Then the value of the camel will be uniquely determined and you can check whether the operation makes sense.

6. SWEET BREAKFAST

Organizing the data visually might help.
How can you obtain the third row from the first two?

![croissant] + ![coffee with heart] + ![coffee with heart] = **$6.60**

![croissant] + ![croissant] + ![coffee] = **$6**

![croissant] + ![coffee with heart] = **?**

7. TRIANGULAR CAT

Remember to count triangles of all sizes.
For instance, in the figure to the right one
can distinguish three different triangles.

8. CROWDED BUS

Be careful about the difference between "passengers" and
"people on the bus".

9. MANY SIBLINGS

There is at least one children in that family: Laura. Keep
adding brothers and sisters until the requirements of the
problems are satisfied.

10. SPIDER'S WEBS

Find the path between the two branches that involves the
minimum possible number of pieces of the web.

11. SONGWRITERS

If you add the five songs to which Pedro contributed to the six songs to which Camila contributed you obtain 11. However, the total number of songs is only 8. What causes this apparent discrepancy?

12. EVEN AND ODD

There are clearly 5 even numbers and 5 odd ones among the numbers from 1 to 10 that are written inside the rectangle. So one can start by writing two 5's in place of the dots. At this point something is off and requires adjusting...

13. CURIOUS BIRTHDAYS

In which months can these birthdays occur? And on which days of each of these months?

14. LACK OF CASH

If Robert had two dollars or more, then the two friends would be able to buy the comic book, since Marina is missing only two dollars.

15. GLOVES OBSESSION

The answer to the problem would be very different if we were talking about socks instead of gloves.

16. MATHEMATICAL WONDERS

The number you are looking for can be obtained by modifying slightly the second number written on the blackboard.

17. HUNGRY MONKEYS

How long does it take a monkey to eat a banana?

18. THREE SPECIAL NUMBERS

No hint for this riddle!

19. STAYING HYDRATED

Let us represent the situation graphically.

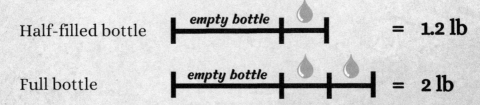

Half-filled bottle   = 1.2 lb

Full bottle   = 2 lb

The goal is to discover the weight of the empty bottle. But first, can you see a way to find the weight of half of the water contained in the bottle, that is, of ?

20. OLD FRIENDS

Let us represent the situation graphically. The older the friend, the longer the segment.

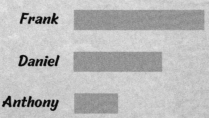

Frank

Daniel

Anthony

Now use the given information on the sum of the ages.

21. IMPERFECT CUTTING

Here is a representation of Nancy's pizza. How many straight cuts do you need at minimum to obtain 11 pieces?

44

22. PRESIDENTIAL RIDDLE

Ask yourself why the sentence in the trivia book is not written as follows: "Of the first **four** US presidents, three died on the fourth of July."

23. UNRELIABLE ANTS

The sentence of the yellow ant implies that the day is either November 29 (in case the yellow ant is telling the truth) or November 30 (in case the yellow ant is lying).

24. SPORT WITH FRIENDS

First compute how many tickets Christian would have to buy in each of the two different scenarios.

25. DIFFICULT MEASUREMENTS

Here is what we obtain if we put the two images one on top of the other.

26. CORDIAL GATHERING

Each person shakes hand with the other eight. In this way, however, every handshake is counted twice.

27. SOCCER CUP

Let us introduce some symbols to make the riddle clearer.

C = goals scored by Chelsea during the first half of the game
c = goals scored by Chelsea during the second half of the game
J = goals scored by Juventus during the first half of the game
j = goals scored by Juventus during the second half of the game

Since Chelsea won 7 - 5, we know that
$C + c = 7$
$J + j = 5$

To solve the riddle, try to formulate the last clue in terms of the symbols just introduced.

28. MEASURING TIME

No hint for this riddle.

29. LOST BANKNOTE

Look at the page numbers of the first book you can find.

30. THIRSTY CAMELS

How often does a Bactrian camel need to drink a gallon of water?

31. WALL PAINTING

What fraction of the wall does each painter complete in one hour? What fraction of the wall is completed in one hour when they work together?

32. ERASE AND WRITE

How many times will Lee carry out this operation of erasing two numbers and writing another one on the blackboard?

33. READY FOR THANKSGIVING

Imagine that every farmer who owns nine turkeys gives four of them to a farmer who has only one. Now it should be easier to count the total number of turkeys.

34. THREATENING QUEENS

Place one queen at a time on the chessboard.

35. LAND DIVISION

Can you see some relation between the long side and the short side of each rectangular piece?

36. THREE CURIOUS FRIENDS

Let us denote each friend with their initial letter. Here is what we know:

$J + L = 27$

$T + J = 30$

$T + L = 33$

We are interested in the quantity $J + L + T$. Is there any way of obtaining it from the three equalities above?

37. PICK AND SUM

What is the smallest possible sum that Ethan can obtain? What is the largest?

38. APPLES AND ORANGES

In the second picture you can replace the two apples with three oranges.

39. TIES ALLOWED

Consider first the possibilities without ties, then those involving a tie in first or second place.

40. STRANGE PLANETS

How many steps must Quke walk to make a progress of one step?

41. GAME OF MARBLES

How many marbles did each friend have before the last game? Try to reason backwards.

42. FAST FOOD

A graphical representation of the situation might help.

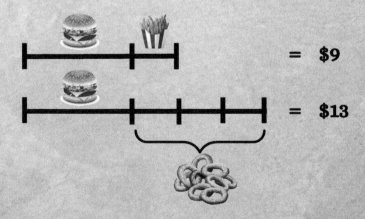

Do you see a way to find out the cost of a portion of fries?

43. OUT FOR A WALK

Try to trace Emily's path in the following drawing.

What is the relation between the total distance covered by Emily and the distance between the two houses?

44. CURSED TREASURE

How many pirates are still alive? How many doubloons did the drunk pirate bring with him to the bottom of the sea?

45. FLYING CARDS

If the first person had found two more baseball cards, the second person four more and the third person three more, then they would all have the exact number of cards required to receive the reward. Here is a graphic representation of the situation. Remember that, since all the cards were recovered, the sum of the three blue pieces is 120.

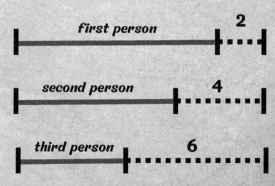

46. HOSPITABLE ISLAND

Reason backwards. How many cookies were in the box before the third pirate ate his share?

47. EFFICIENT CHAINS

Mark does not need to open rings on all four pieces.

48. FAST SALES

Reason backwards. Gloria had six watermelons before the last customer came. How many did she have before the second customer?

49. STOLEN BERRIES

Consider the sentence "A bird has eaten 2 out of every 7 of her berries." For it to make sense, the total number of berries must be a multiple of 7.

50. BEDTIME STORY

The first digit of the two numbers cannot be the same. In fact, if that was the case, **the sum of all four digits would be an odd number.** Can you figure out why?
Since the sum is 24, that is, an even number, we only need to check the pairs 19-20, 29-30, 39-40, and so on.

51. GROWING BACTERIA

How are the two scenarios related? At what time were there three bacteria in Matilde's test tube?

52. WEEKEND IN SPACE

In the end, each of the four remaining spaceships has the same number of passengers. What is this number? Remember that it is the smallest possible.

53. SCOUTING CAMPAIGN

What distance will the company travel in three hours?

54. CHEERFUL BIRDS

How many birds went away without coming back to the tree? How many birds were on the tree initially?

55. BIRTHDAY PARTY

You might find it useful to use the following diagram, where the first guest is represented by the number 1, the second by the number 2, and so on. A line between two people means that they know each other. The lines connecting the guests to Patrick have already been drawn. It is up to you to draw the missing lines.

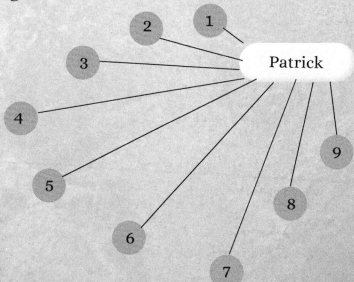

56. MATH MAGICIAN

5482+4517=9999. Similarly, 1450+8549=9999.

57. ASTEROID IMPACT

How far from the Earth's surface will the asteroid be when the rocket ship takes off?

58. MARTIAN MISSION

After the second break:

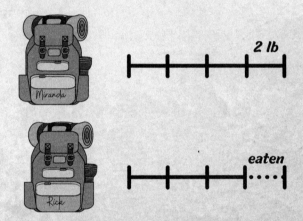

After the first break:

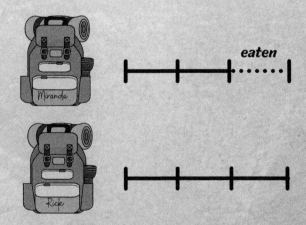

59. HUNGRY PUPPIES

How many croquettes do the puppies eat in a second between the four of them? How many croquettes are there in total?

60. DESERT CROSSING

The first step is taking trips to a spot one hour away and deposit some fuel tanks there.

ANSWERS

1. SECRET CODE

Here is the secret code.

$$1 \quad 6 \quad 3$$

As we have seen in the hint, it was convenient to start from the information on the product. In fact, there are always less ways to obtain a given number as a product than there are to obtain it as a sum. For instance, consider the number 12. There are only 3 pairs of natural numbers whose product is 12 (1 and 12, 2 and 6, 3 and 4). However, there are 7 pairs of numbers whose sum is 12 (can you see which ones? Remember that the first natural number is 0).

The Little Mathematician

Find a formula that, given any natural number, immediately tells you how many pairs of natural numbers have the chosen number as their sum. With that formula, you will be able to answer in a few seconds a question like the following one:

How many pairs of numbers have 1246 as their sum?

Hints:
- Start with some examples. Do you notice a pattern?
- Be careful of the difference between odd and even numbers.

2. MYSTERIOUS WEIGHT

The fifth weight measures 10 lb.

Since the total weight is an even number, the fifth weight can only measure 2 lb or 10 lb. If it were 2 lb, then the sum of the five weights would be 22 lb, and therefore there would be 11 lb on each side of the scale. This is clearly impossible to obtain with the given weights. Therefore, we conclude that the fifth weight measures 10 lb. In the next page, you can see how the balanced scale looks like.

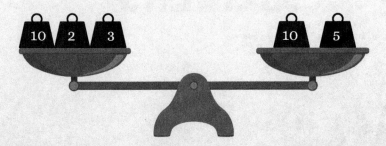

3. PERFECT BBQ

It takes Frank 15 minutes to grill the three steaks.
Let us call the steaks A, B, and C. Then
5 minutes: first side of A, first side of B;
5 minutes: second side of A, first side of C;
5 minutes: second side of B; second side of C.

4. GIGANTIC PRODUCTS

The last digit of the result is 0. The one before last is also 0.
Since among the factors there are the numbers 10, 100, and 1000, the product will end with quite a few zeros.

The Little Mathematician

Here is a different version of the same problem. Suppose that the teacher had focused on odd numbers instead, and asked

What is the last digit of the following product?

1 x 3 x 5 x 7 x.....x 2023

Can you find the answer to this question? Can you come up with other gigantic products of which you can predict the last digit? Use them to trick your friends and teachers!

5. CHALLENGE FROM THE DESERT

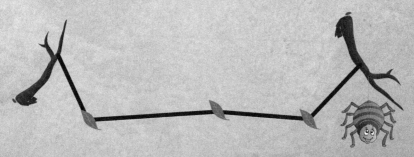 = 4   ▲ = 8

6. SWEET BREAKFAST

I spent $4.20 for my croissant and cappuccino.
Between Alyssa and Jasmine, they consumed three cappuccinos and three croissants, spending a total of $12.60. The cost of one croissant and one cappuccino is therefore $12.60/3 = $4.20.

7. TRIANGULAR CAT

In James's drawing one can count a total of 17 triangles.

8. CROWDED BUS

Only one person was left on the bus: the driver.

9. MANY SIBLINGS

At minimum, Laura has one sister and two brothers.
If Laura had only one brother, that child would not be able to say that he has at least one brother and one sister.

10. SPIDER'S WEBS

The storm destroyed at most 18 pieces of the web.
Since the shortest path between the branches consists of four pieces of the web, the storm destroyed at most 22-4=18 pieces.

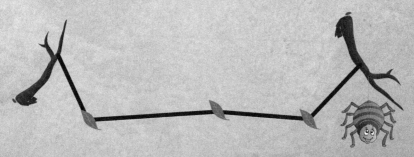

11. SONGWRITERS

Pedro and Camila wrote 3 songs together.
Let us represent the situation with a diagram.

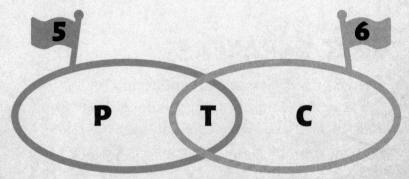

P = Songs written by Pedro alone.

C = Songs written by Camila alone.

T = Songs written by Camila and Pedro together.

Here is what we know from the riddle.

$$\left.\begin{array}{l} P+T=5 \\ C+T=6 \end{array}\right\} \quad P+T+C+T=11$$

$$P+C+T=8$$

In the sum 5+6=11, the songs written together by Camila and Pedro are counted twice. Therefore, the number of songs written together is 11-8=3.

The Little Mathematician

Write your own math riddle that exploits the same principles. It will start like this:

In a classroom of 23 students each plays at least one sport between basketball and baseball...

12. EVEN AND ODD

1	2	3	4

Inside this rectangle there are 7 odd numbers.

5	6

Inside this rectangle there are 5 even numbers.

7	8	9	10

The Little Mathematician

Invent **your own tricky rectangle**, with some number of your choice along the edges and the following two sentences inside:

Inside this rectangle there are ... multiples of 3.

Inside this rectangle there are ... multiples of 5.

<u>Warning</u>: Not every random choice of numbers will give a rectangle that has a solution.

13. CURIOUS BIRTHDAYS

There are at most 75 friends.

There are 13 possible birthdays in each of the following months: January, March, October and December. There are 11 possible birthdays in February and 12 in November. The total number of possibilities is 13x4+11+12=75.

14. LACK OF CASH

The comic book costs $7.

Since after adding Robert's dollar bills Marina still does not have enough to buy the comic book, Robert has only one dollar in his pocket. He needs 6 more dollars to buy the comic book, which therefore costs $7.

15. GLOVES OBSESSION

Samantha must pick at least 31 gloves.
The worst-case scenario is when she first picks all 30 right (or left) gloves. Surprisingly, the different colors do not matter in this problem.

16. MATHEMATICAL WONDERS

The number is 371.
In this riddle you discovered three numbers that are equal to the sum of the third powers of their digits. You could ask what happens if we replace the third power with a second power. That is, we ask the following question:

> *What are the numbers that are equal to*
> *the sum of the squares of their digits?*

Do not waste time in trying to find such numbers! Mathematicians have proved that the only numbers with this property are 0 and 1.

17. HUNGRY MONKEYS

It takes 14 monkeys to eat 98 bananas in 49 minutes.
Since 7 monkeys eat 7 bananas in 7 minutes, one monkey eats a banana in 7 minutes. Therefore in 49 minutes one monkey eats 7 bananas. We conclude that we need 98/7=14 monkeys to eat 98 bananas in 49 minutes.

18. THREE SPECIAL NUMBERS

The special numbers are 1,2, and 3.
Can you now find four special numbers? That is, can you find four numbers whose product is equal to their sum?

19. STAYING HYDRATED

The empty bottle weighs 0.4 lb.
The difference 2 lb - 1.2 lb = 0.8 lb corresponds to half of the water that the bottle can contain. Therefore the weight of the empty bottle is 1.2 lb - 0.8 lb = 0.4 lb.

20. OLD FRIENDS

Robert is the oldest, while Anthony is the youngest.
Since Frank and Daniel are both older than Anthony, the only way in which the sum of their ages is less than the sum of the ages of Anthony and Robert, is if Robert is the oldest.

21. IMPERFECT CUTTING

Nancy made at least four cuts.
To the right is an example of how four cuts can produce eleven pieces. We do not recommend trying this on your pizza.

The Little Mathematician

We have seen that a pizza can be cut into 11 parts with four straight cuts. With four cuts it is impossible to obtain more pieces. What is the maximum number of pieces (not necessarily of the same shape or size) that can be obtained with three cuts? And with five? Fill the table below. Do you notice any pattern?

Number of straight cuts	2	3	4	5	6	7
Maximum number of pieces	...	...	11	...	...	...

22. PRESIDENTIAL RIDDLE

If Monroe had not died on July 4, then he would not have been included. In that case, Simon would have read in his trivia book that, of the first **four** US presidents, three died on the fourth of July.

23. UNRELIABLE ANTS

The conversation took place on November 30.
As explained in the hint, the sentence of the yellow ant implies that it is either November 29 or November 30. Since we are in one of the last two days of the month, the red ant is telling the truth.

24. SPORT WITH FRIENDS

It is cheaper to take 10 friends to a basketball game.
To take 10 friends to a basketball game, Christian would have to buy in total 11 tickets. To take 4 friends to 5 different hockey games, he would have to buy a total of 25 tickets. Since 11 basketball tickets cost the same as 22 hockey tickets, the basketball game is the cheaper option.

25. DIFFICULT MEASUREMENTS

The height of the table is 35 inches.
Putting the two images on top of each other shows that 70 inches corresponds to twice the height of the table (see the hint).

26. CORDIAL GATHERING

There were in total 36 handshakes.
Each participant shook hands with the other eight. In this way, however, every handshake is counted twice. Therefore, the total number of handshakes is (9x8)/2 = 36.

We can also reason in the following way. The first participants shakes hands with the other eight. Then the second participant shakes hands with seven others (having already shaken hands with the first person), and so on.

The total number of handshakes is therefore $8+7+6+...+1 = 36$.

The Little Mathematician

How many handshakes are there if the participants are more than nine? Fill the table below. Can you notice a pattern?

Number of people	9	10	11	12	13	14
Number of handshakes	36	...	...	...	...	...

What if there are 120 participants?

27. SOCCER CUP

During the first half of the game 5 goals were scored.

Using the symbols introduced in the hint, we have the equalities $C + c = 7$ and $J + j = 5$. Moreover, since Chelsea scored in the first half of the game as many goals as Juventus scored in the second half of the game, we have that $C = j$.

The riddle asks for the total number of goals scored during the first half of the game, that is, the quantity $C + J$.

We have that $C + J = j + J = 5$.

28. MEASURING TIME

Start the two hourglasses at the same time. After 4 minutes, turn the 4-minute one upside down. Do the same after 7 minutes with the other one. When the 4-minute hourglass stops for the second time, 8 minutes have passed. The 7-minute hourglass has been running for only 1 minute. Therefore, it is enough to turn it upside down to measure one additional minute.

29. LOST BANKNOTE

I gave the banknote to the woman.

It is impossible to stick a banknote between the pages 201 and 202 of a book since they are two sides of the same sheet of paper.

30. THIRSTY CAMELS

The Bactrian camel requires a higher daily amount of water.

A Bactrian camel drinks one gallon of water every 5 days, while an Arabian camel drinks one gallon of water every 7 days. Therefore, a Bactrian camel has a higher daily consumption of water.

31. WALL PAINTING

It will take Levin and Alex two hours to paint the wall.

Levin paints 1/3 of the wall in one hour, while Alex paints 1/6 of the wall in one hour. When working together, in one hour they are able to complete 1/3 + 1/6 = 3/6 of the wall. Therefore, they will complete the job in two hours.

32. ERASE AND WRITE

The number left on the blackboard is 64.

In fact, 64 is the sum of the numbers from 1 to 10 (1+2+3+...+10=55) plus 9, which is the number of times the cancellation has been performed.

33. READY FOR THANKSGIVING

In that community there are 100 turkeys.

Suppose that each farmer who has 9 turkeys gave 4 turkeys to a farmer who only has one. Then every farmer in the community would have 5 turkeys. Since there are 20 farmers, the total number of turkeys is 5x20=100.

The Little Mathematician

Note that we still do not know how many farmers own 9 turkeys, and there is no way for us to know it. This is the power of the mathematical concept of **average**. An equivalent (but easier) formulation for this riddle could have been:

> *In a community of 20 turkey farmers, each farmer has on average 5 turkeys. How many turkeys are there in total?*

Use your mastery of the concept of average to invent a tricky riddle about a town of 1,000 people where each person owns one car, two cars, or no cars.

34. THREATENING QUEENS

On a 3x3 chessboard the problem has no solution. Here is a possible configuration for the 4x4 case.

35. LAND DIVISION

The area of the land is 4,800 square feet.

From the picture, one sees that in every rectangular piece the long side is three times the short side. Therefore, the perimeter is equal to 8 times the short side. Hence the short side measures 20 ft, the long side 60 ft, and the total area is 20x60x4=4,800 square feet.

36. THREE CURIOUS FRIENDS

The three friends found a total of 45 insects. Thomas is the one who found the highest number of insects.

If you sum the three given numbers, the contribution of each friend is counted twice. Therefore, the total number of insects found by the three friends is (27+30+33)/2=45. Thomas found more insects than his friends since his name appears in the two highest sums given in the problem.

37. PICK AND SUM

Ethan can obtain 4015 different sums.

The smallest possible sum is 13+14=27, while the largest one is 2020+2021=4041. All the numbers in between these two are clearly obtainable. So, how many numbers are there between 27 and 4041? It is like counting to 4041, but neglecting the first 26 numbers. Therefore, there are 4041-26=4015 numbers.

38. APPLES AND ORANGES

An apple weighs 1.5 lb.

Replacing two apples with three oranges in the second picture we obtain the following:

Removing two oranges and 1 lb from each side, the scale remains balanced, and we see that the weight of an orange is 1 lb. Now one can look at the first picture in the riddle an conclude that an apple weighs 1.5 lb.

39. TIES ALLOWED

The race can end in thirteen different ways.

There are six ways in which the race can end without ties. Then three possibilities involve a tie in first place (corresponding to the three options for the person who finishes third) and three more involve a tie in second place. Finally, there is also the possibility that they all get to the finishing line at the same exact time.

40. STRANGE PLANETS

Quke is 20 steps away from his front door.

Every five steps, Quke moves forward by one. Therefore, after 100 steps, he is 100/5=20 steps away from his front door.

41. GAME OF MARBLES

Before the first game one friend had 35 marbles and the other 77.
Before the third game one of them had 56/2=28 marbles, while the other had 56+28=84 marbles. Before the second game one of them had 84/2=42 marbles, while the other had 28+42=70 marbles. Before the first game one had 70/2=35 marbles while the other had 42+35=77 marbles.

42. FAST FOOD

A cheeseburger costs $7.
The difference between the two given prices is $4, and it corresponds to twice the price of the regular fries (see the hint). Hence the fries cost $2 and the cheeseburger costs $7.

43. OUT FOR A WALK

The distance between the two houses is eight miles.
The detour taken by Emily amounts to half of the distance between the two houses. Indeed, she walked one quarter of the distance toward her own house, and then the same distance back to the point where she had decided to turn around. Hence 12 miles correspond to 1.5 times the distance between the houses.

44. CURSED TREASURE

After the initial distribution of the treasure, each pirate had 100 doubloons.
There are only 5 surviving pirates, and thus a total of 350x5=1750 doubloons. Before the last two men died, that sum was divided among seven pirates, that is, each of them had 1750/7=250 doubloons. Therefore, 250 doubloons disappeared into the sea with the drunk pirate. It follows that the entire treasure consisted of 2000 doubloons. Therefore, each pirate had 2000/20=100 doubloons initially.

45. FLYING CARDS

To receive the reward, one had to find 44 cards.

If we add to the 120 cards brought by the three people the number of cards they were missing to get the reward, we obtain 120+2+4+6=132. This number corresponds to exactly three times the quantity that would have granted the reward. Therefore, the number we are looking for is 132/3=44.

46. HOSPITABLE ISLAND

At the beginning there were 39 cookies in the box.

In the morning there are 4 cookies. Before the last pirate woke up there were 4x2+1= 9 cookies. Before the second pirate woke up there were 9x2+1=19 cookies. At the beginning there were 19x2+1=39 cookies.

47. EFFICIENT CHAINS

It will take Mark 6 minutes to make the chain.

Mark opens all three rings in one of the chain pieces and uses them to connect the remaining three pieces together.

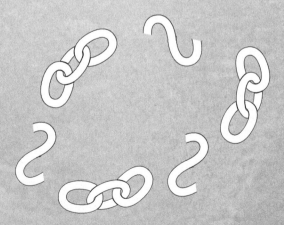

48. FAST SALES

At the beginning of the day Gloria had 18 watermelons.

Before the second customer bought one third of the watermelons, Gloria had nine. Since the first customer bought half of her initial number of watermelons, she had 18 at the beginning.

49. STOLEN BERRIES

When she got home, Kayla had 28 berries in her basket.

The only multiples of 7 between 16 and 40 are 21, 28, and 35. After the bird has eaten 2 out of every 7, the number of remaining berries in each case would be 15, 20, and 25, respectively. The number of berries left must be even since they are evenly split between strawberries and blueberries. Therefore, 20 is the correct alternative. We conclude that, when she got home, Kayla had 28 berries in her basket.

50. BEDTIME STORY

Grandma read pages 79 and 80.

51. GROWING BACTERIA

The test tube would have been full at 4.30 pm.

In the first scenario, the test tube contains three bacteria at 8.30 am. Hence the second situation is the same as the first just half an hour ahead.

The Little Mathematician

Write your own riddle about a microorganism that doubles in size every hour.

52. WEEKEND IN SPACE

Each spaceship returns to Gok with 22 passengers.

Since 22-17=5, 22-19=3, and 22-14=8, the fifth spaceship had 5+3+8=16 passengers.

53. SCOUTING CAMPAIGN

Misty will have to turn around after 2.5 hours.

In three hours, the platoon walks 12 miles. Misty can cover those 12 miles in the first two hours. To make sure she is on that exact spot after one more hour, she should move forward for 30 minutes and then turn around.

54. CHEERFUL BIRDS

There were at most 14 Robins on the cherry tree.

At the beginning there were 17 birds in total (the 13 that are there now plus the 4 that flew away without coming back). Since we know that at least 3 of the birds initially on the tree were Cardinals, the maximum possible number of Robins is 14.

55. BIRTHDAY PARTY

Lauren knows 5 people: Patrick, plus four other guests.

In Patrick's list, these four guests correspond to the numbers 5, 6, 7, and 8.

56. MATH MAGICIAN

Lucas's numbers are based on the first two numbers chosen by the "victim" of the trick. To obtain his numbers, Lucas simply subtracts from 9 every single digit of the first two numbers written on the board. For instance, if the first two numbers given by the victim are 5711 and 3168, Lucas says 4288 and 6831. The sum of these four numbers is 9999+9999=19,998. Thanks to Lucas's carefully chosen numbers, this sum will always be 19,998.

To find the sum of all the five numbers on the board, Malika only has to look at the third number chosen by the victim and add 19,998, which is easy: just add 20,000 and then subtract 2.

57. ASTEROID IMPACT

When the head of the EADD pushes the button to initiate the 10 second countdown for the launch, the asteroid is 114 miles from the Earth.

It takes the rocket ship 2 seconds to travel 6 miles. In those 2 seconds, the asteroid travels 18 miles. Therefore, when the rocket ship takes off, the asteroid must be 6+18=24 miles from Earth. Ten seconds earlier, the asteroid is 24+90=114 miles from the surface of the Earth.

58. MARTIAN MISSION

When Rick and Miranda started their ascent of Olympus Mons, each of them was carrying a backpack of the weight of 9.6 lb.

From the first picture in the hint, we see that Rick and Miranda, before the second break, carried a total of 16 lb, that is, 8 lb each. Recall that, after the first break, the situation was as follows:

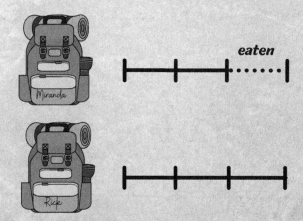

Since what is left after eating must be equal to 16 lb, we conclude that, in the first break, Rick and Miranda consumed 16/5 = 3.2 lb of food. The initial weight of a backpack was 3.2 x 3 = 9.6 lb.

59. HUNGRY PUPPIES

It will take the puppies 200 seconds to finish all the food.
In total, there are 140+120+120+120=500 croquettes. Every second the puppies eat 1+0.5+0.5+0.5=2.5 croquettes. Therefore, it will take them 500/2.5=200 seconds to finish all the food.

60. DESERT CROSSING

The most efficient strategy allows Beatrix to cross the desert in 15 hours.
The first step is taking trips to a spot one hour away and deposit tanks there. She should do this four times. Here is the situation after eight hours.

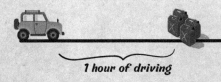

1 hour of driving

Beatrix can now drive one hour (obviously starting with three hours' worth of fuel), refill after one hour, and deposit a tank in a spot one hour further away. Here is the situation three hours after the previous picture (note that the jeep contains no fuel at this time).

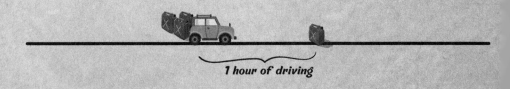

1 hour of driving

Beatrix can now start with fuel for three hours, stop after one hour to refuel, and then drive the remaining three hours to finish the crossing of the desert.
The total time is 8+3+4=15 hours.

DID YOU ENJOY THIS BOOK?

Buy now on Amazon our collection of logic puzzles

Logic Grid Puzzles & Other Games: A Fun and Challenging Logic Workbook for Kids 8-12

YOUR FREE GIFT

We hope you enjoyed this collection of math riddles.

As a way of saying thank you for your purchase, we would like to offer you for FREE the ebook **12 Tricky Brain Teasers to enjoy with Family and Friends.**

Scan this QR code to receive your free gift now!

$12 \times 84 = 1008$

$134 \times 12 = 1608$

$2346 \times 12 =$

Printed in Great Britain
by Amazon

19744870R00045